HAL LEONARD PIANO REPERTOIRE
Book 2 • Late Elementary

JOURNEY THROUGH THE
CLASSICS

COMPILED AND EDITED BY JENNIFER LINN

Journey Through the Classics is a four-volume piano repertoire series designed to lead students seamlessly from the easiest classics to the intermediate masterworks. The graded pieces are presented in a progressive order and feature a variety of classical favorites essential to any piano student's educational foundation. The authentic repertoire is ideal for auditions and recitals and each book includes a handy reference chart with the key, composer, stylistic period, and challenge elements listed for each piece.

-Jennifer Linn

Dedicated in loving memory to my mother and first teacher,
Geraldine Ruth Ryan Lange.

Cover art: Rose Garden, 1876 (oil on canvas) by Claude Monet (1840-1926)
Private Collection/ Photo © Lefevre Fine Art Ltd., London/ The Bridgeman Art Library
Nationality / copyright status: French / out of copyright
Adaptation by Jen McClellan

ISBN 978-1-4584-1150-1

HAL•LEONARD®
CORPORATION
7777 W. BLUEMOUND RD. P.O. BOX 13819 MILWAUKEE, WI 53213

In Australia Contact:
Hal Leonard Australia Pty. Ltd.
4 Lentara Court
Cheltenham, Victoria, 3192 Australia
Email: ausadmin@halleonard.com.au

Visit Hal Leonard Online at
www.halleonard.com

JOURNEY THROUGH THE CLASSICS:
Book 2 Reference Chart

✔ WHEN COMPLETED	PAGE	TITLE	COMPOSER	ERA	KEY	METER	CHALLENGE ELEMENTS
	4	Russian Folk Song	Beethoven	Classical	G	$\frac{2}{4}$	Dotted rhythm; legato/staccato coordination
	5	Sonatina in C	Duncombe	Baroque	C	$\frac{2}{4}$	Triplet and duplet rhythms; RH finger substitution
	6	Minuet in G	Telemann	Baroque	G	$\frac{3}{4}$	Triplet and duplet rhythms; portato touch
	7	Menuet in F	Mozart, L.	Classical	F	$\frac{3}{4}$	Hand shifts; LH octaves; echo dynamics
	8	Trumpet Tune	Duncombe	Baroque	C	$\frac{3}{4}$	Repeated notes and harmonic thirds; hand position extension
	10	Waltz	Vogel	Romantic	G	$\frac{3}{4}$	Balance between melody & accompaniment; connecting pedal
	12	Little Sonata	Wilton	Classical	C	$\frac{4}{4}$ & $\frac{3}{4}$	Accents; syncopation; echo dynamics; RH/LH coordination
	14	Melody (Arabian Air)	Le Couppey	Romantic	Am	$\frac{2}{4}$	Legato touch; phrasing; 16th notes; fermata
	16	Minuet in G	Bach, J.S.	Baroque	G	$\frac{3}{4}$	Articulation; contrapuntal skills; crossing 3 over 1
	18	Morning Prayer	Gurlitt	Romantic	C	¢	Vertical reading; Connecting pedal; both hands in 𝄞
	20	Bagatelle	Diabelli	Classical	C	$\frac{3}{8}$	3/8 time signature; balance between melody & accompaniment
	21	Tarantella	Lynes	Romantic	Am	$\frac{6}{8}$	6/8 time signature; fast legato scales in RH/staccato in LH
	22	Giga	Arnold	Classical	C	$\frac{6}{8}$	Fast and continuous scale patterns in RH
	24	Musette	Le Couppey	Romantic	G	¢	Drone bass; articulation; RH scale patterns with finger crossings
	26	Scotch Dance	Kuhlau	Classical	C	$\frac{2}{4}$	Alberti bass; sforzando chords; coordination between hands
	27	Burleske	Mozart, L.	Classical	G	$\frac{2}{4}$	Broken LH octaves; 16th notes; articulation
	28	Menuet in G	Petzold	Baroque	G	$\frac{3}{4}$	Articulation; finger crossing and contrapuntal skills
	30	Menuet in F	Mozart, W.A.	Classical	F	$\frac{3}{4}$	Finger substitution; articulation; triplet rhythm
	32	Church Bells	Camidge	Classical	C	$\frac{2}{4}$	Vertical reading; connecting pedal; both hands in 𝄞
	33	Bright Sky	Gurlitt	Romantic	C	$\frac{2}{4}$	Alberti bass with shifts; both hands in 𝄞; repeated notes
	36	Sad at Heart	Fuchs	Romantic	Am	$\frac{3}{4}$	Phrasing and balance; pedal; voicing; expression
	37	Sarabande	Pachelbel	Baroque	B♭	$\frac{4}{4}$	B-flat Key signature; vertical reading; connecting pedal
	38	Distant Bells	Streabbog	Romantic	C	$\frac{4}{4}$	Crossing LH over RH; connecting pedal; accents; balance
	40	Night Escape	Gurlitt	Romantic	Dm	$\frac{4}{4}$	LH melody with RH repeating harmonic seconds and thirds

CONTENTS

Russian Folk Song

Ludwig van Beethoven
(1770–1827)

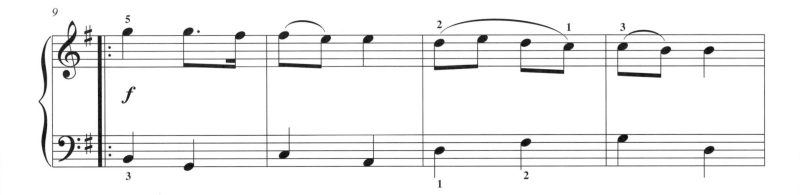

Sonatina in C Major

William Duncombe
(1690–1769)

Minuet in G Major

Georg Philipp Telemann
(1681–1767)

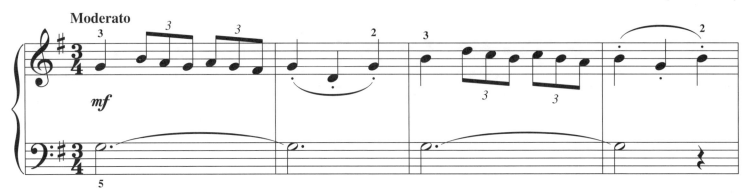

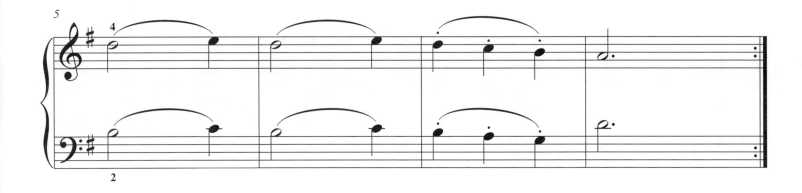

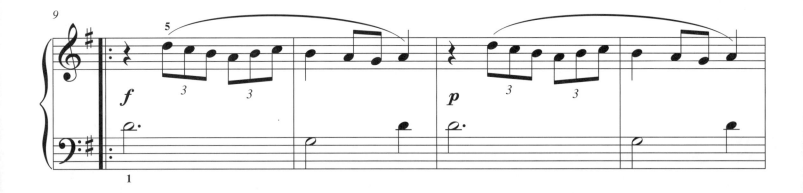

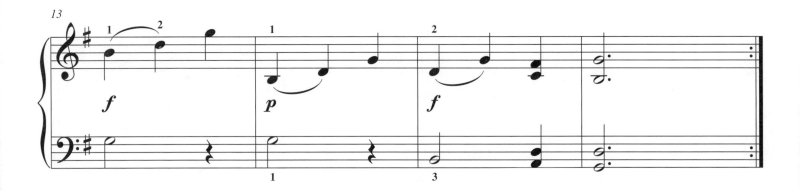

Menuet in F Major

Leopold Mozart
(1719–1787)

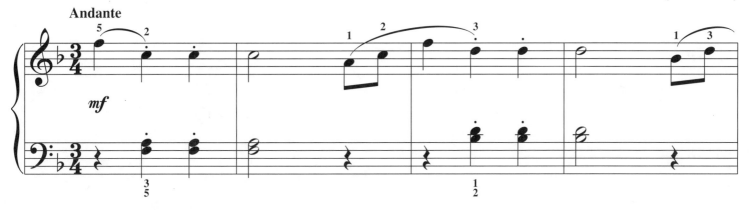

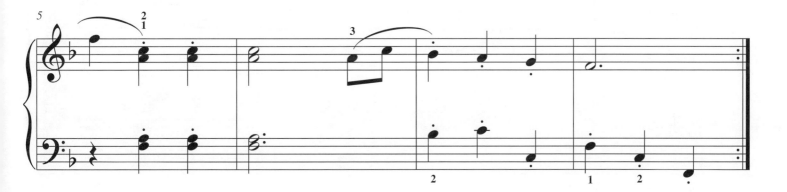

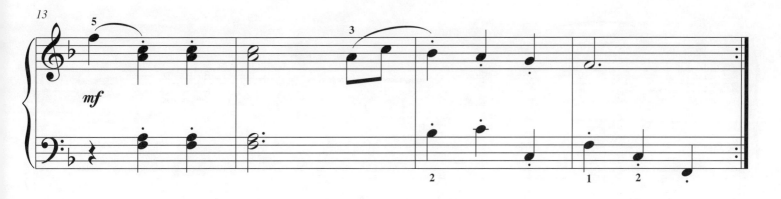

Trumpet Tune

William Duncombe
(1690-1769)

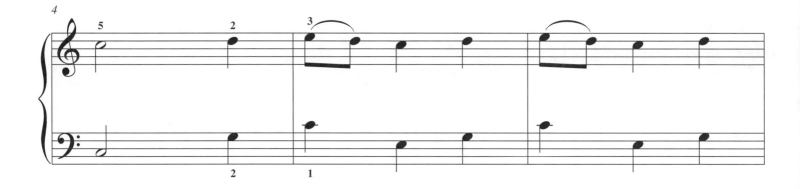

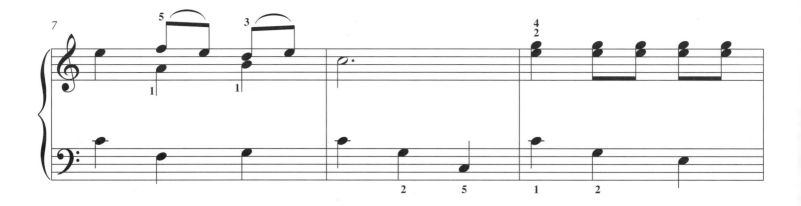

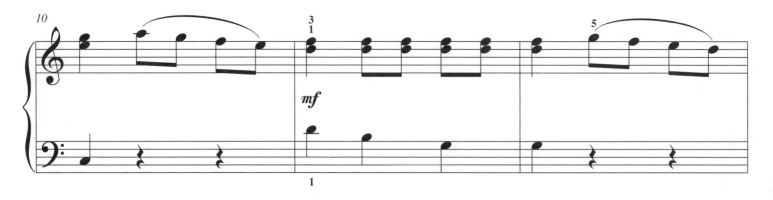

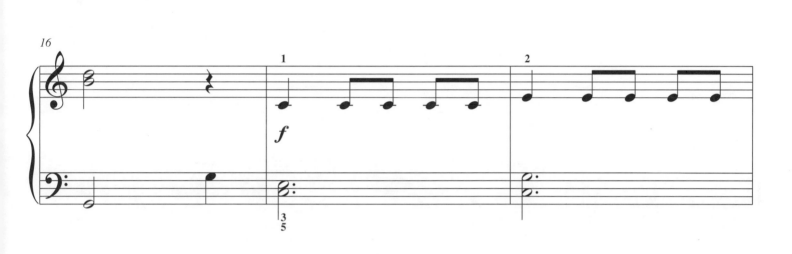

Waltz

Moritz Vogel
(1846–1922)

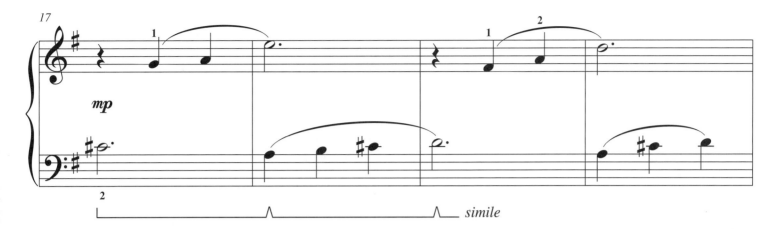

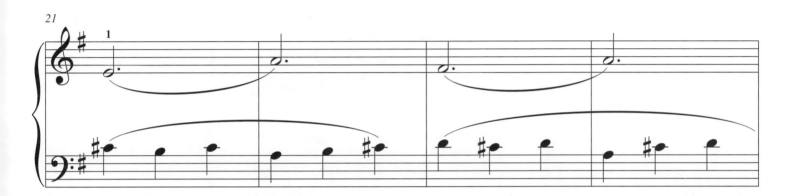

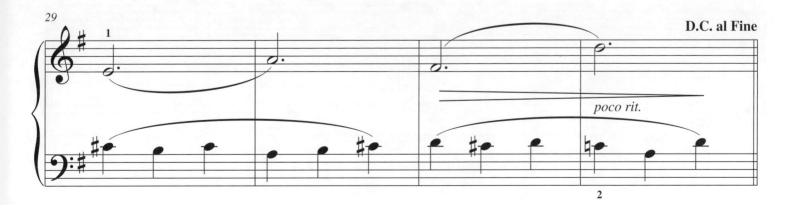

Little Sonata

I.

Charles H. Wilton
(1761–1832)

II.

Minuet
Andante

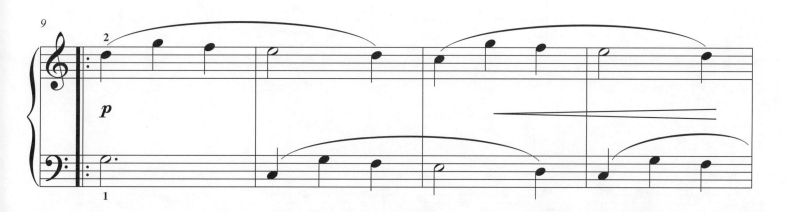

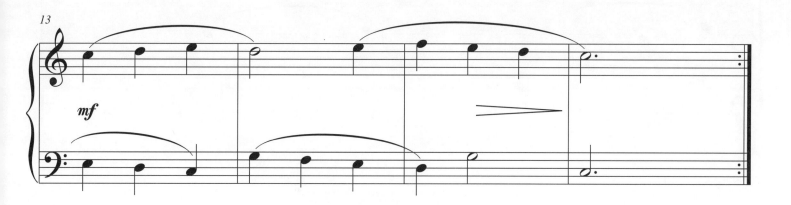

Melody
(Arabian Air)

Félix Le Couppey
(1811–1887)

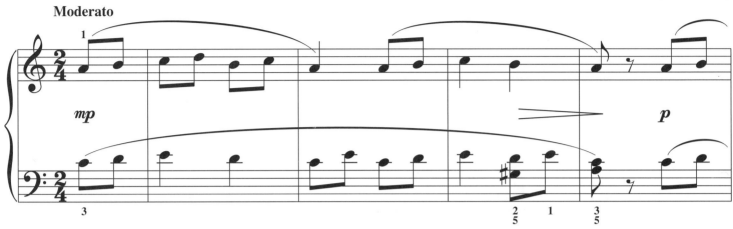

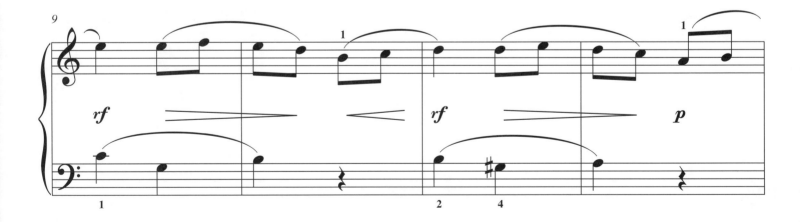

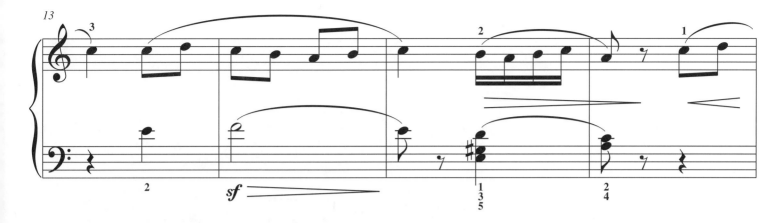

Minuet in G Major
BWV 822

Johann Sebastian Bach
(1685–1750)

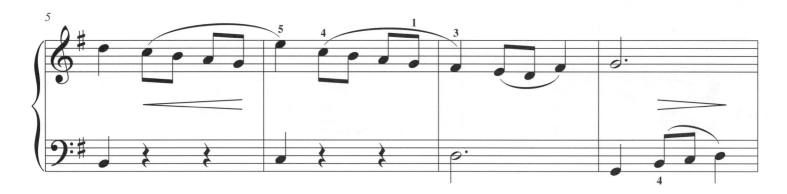

Morning Prayer

Op. 101, No. 2

Cornelius Gurlitt
(1820–1901)

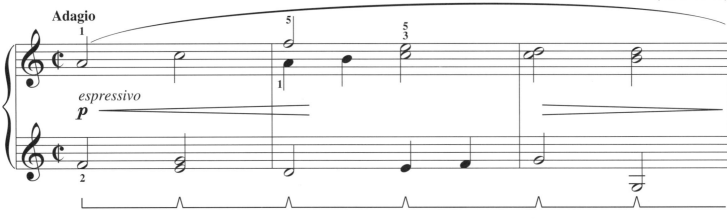

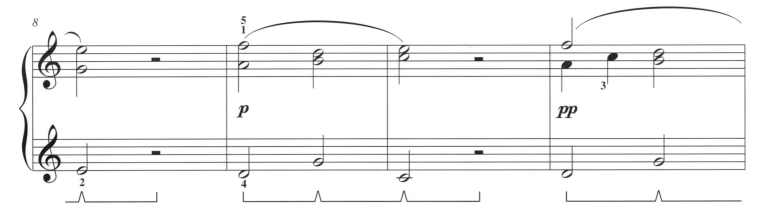

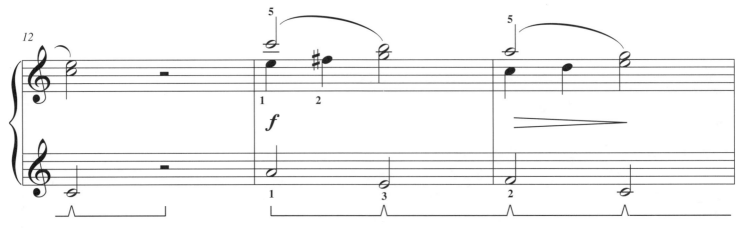

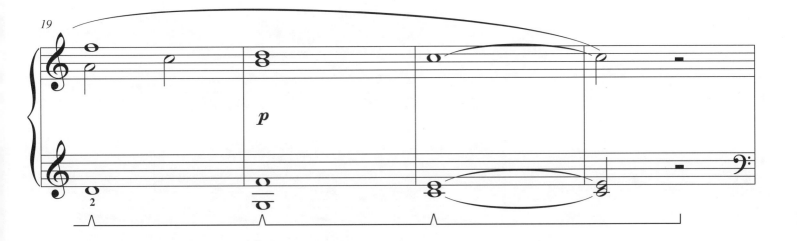

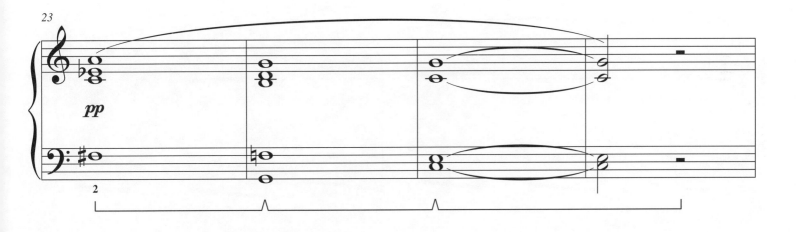

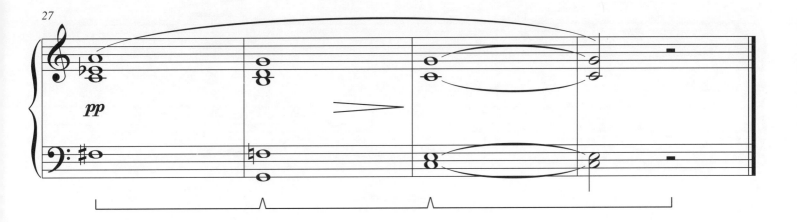

Bagatelle

Anton Diabelli
(1781–1858)

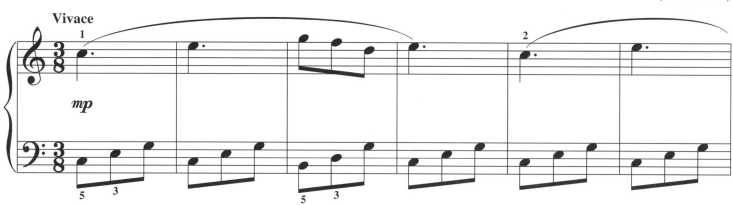

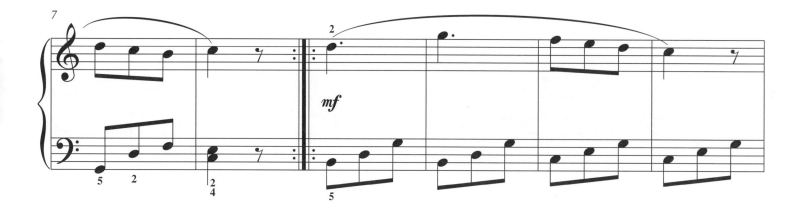

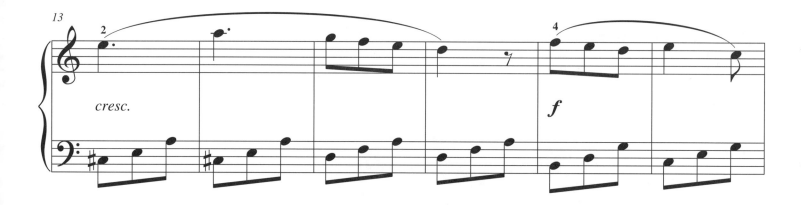

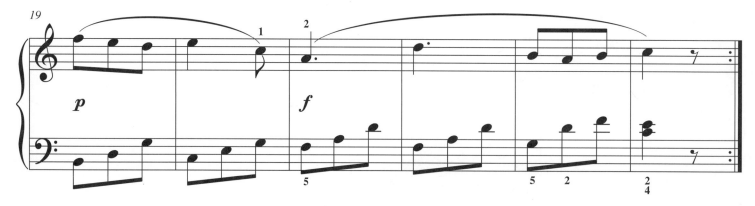

Tarantella
Op. 14, No. 8

Frank Lynes
(1858–1913)

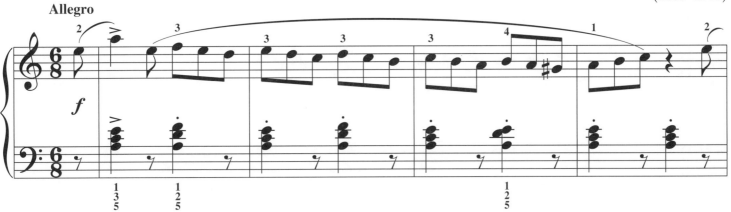

Giga

Samuel Arnold
(1740–1802)

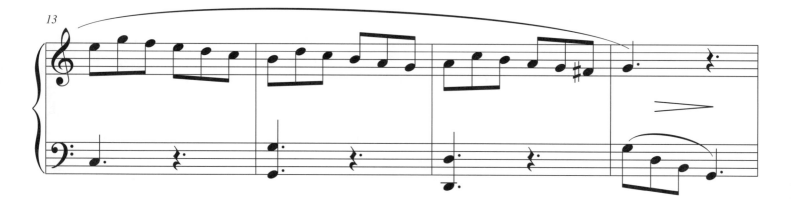

Musette

Félix Le Couppey
(1811-1887)

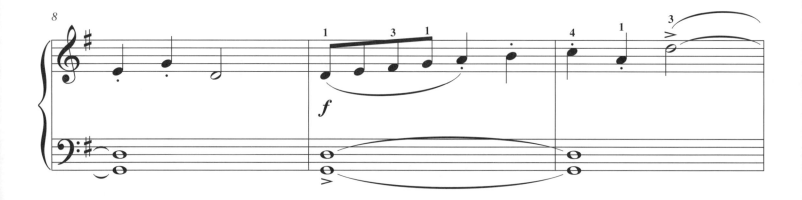

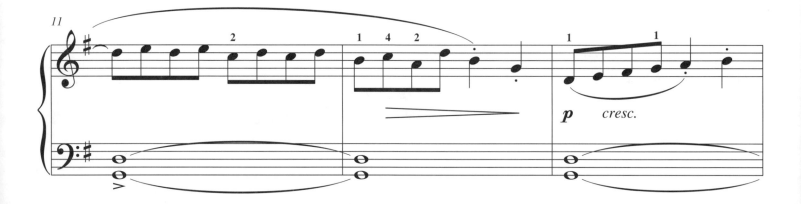

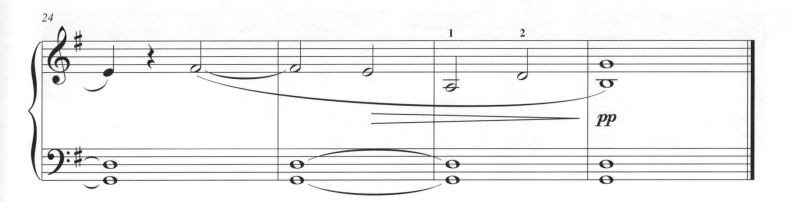

Scotch Dance

Friedrich Kuhlau
(1787–1832)

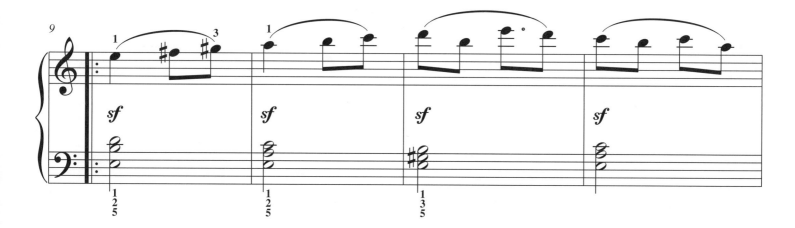

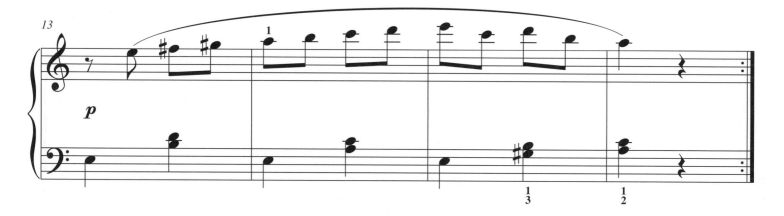

Burleske

Leopold Mozart
(1719-1787)

Menuet in G Major

Christian Petzold
(1677–1733)

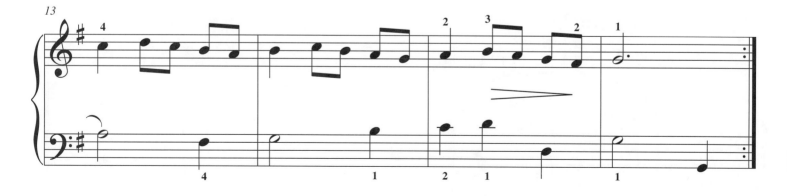

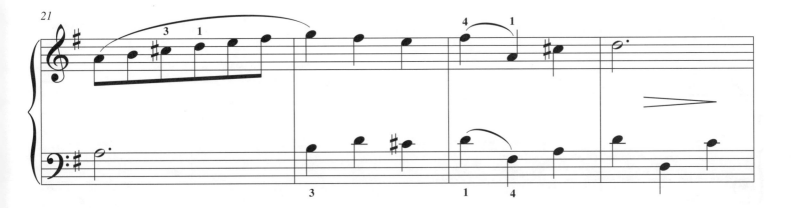

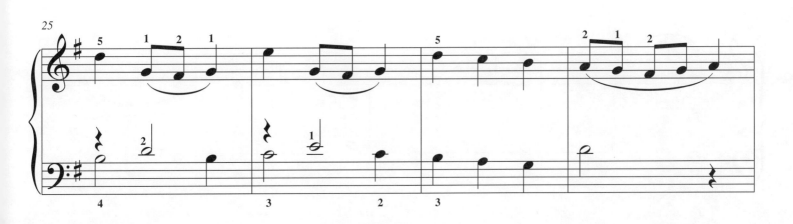

Menuet in F Major

Wolfgang Amadeus Mozart
(1756–1791)

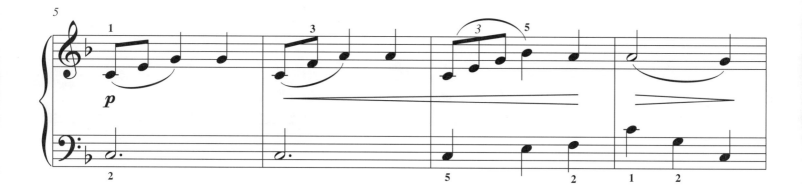

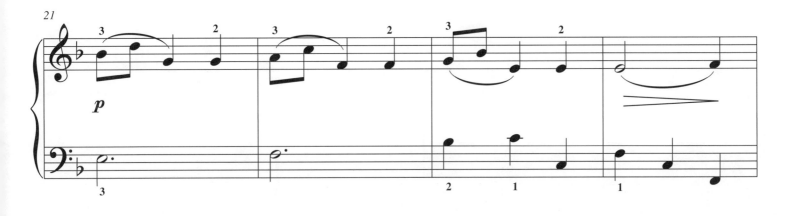

Church Bells

Matthew Camidge
(1758–1844)

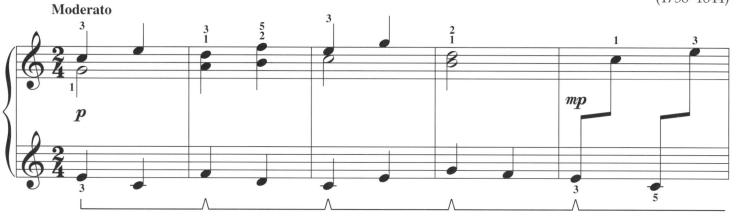

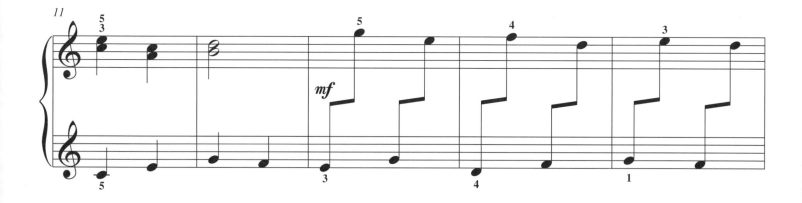

Bright Sky
(Op. 140, No. 3)

Cornelius Gurlitt
(1820-1901)

Allegretto grazioso

Sad at Heart
Op. 47, No. 5

Robert Fuchs
(1847–1927)

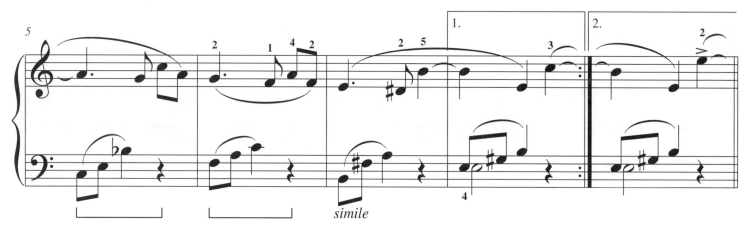

Sarabande

Johann Pachelbel
(1653–1706)

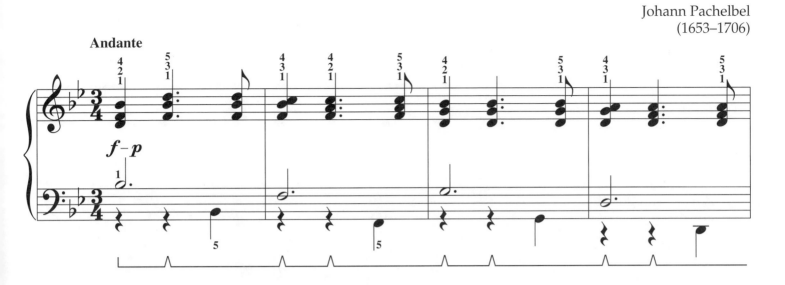

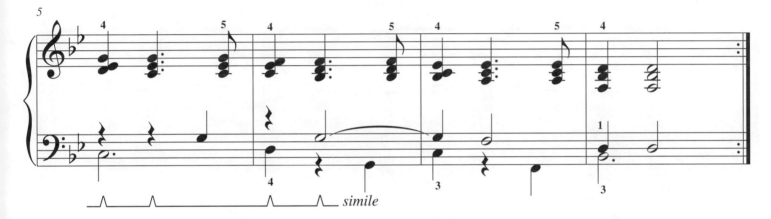

Distant Bells

Op. 63, No. 6

Louis Streabbog
(1835-1886)

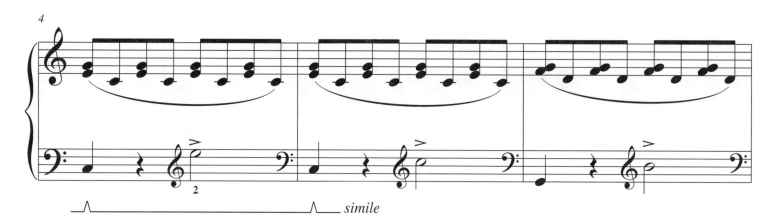

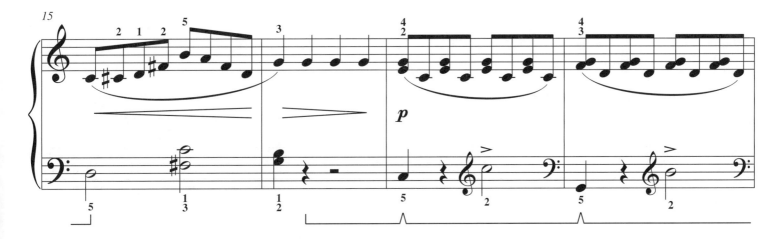

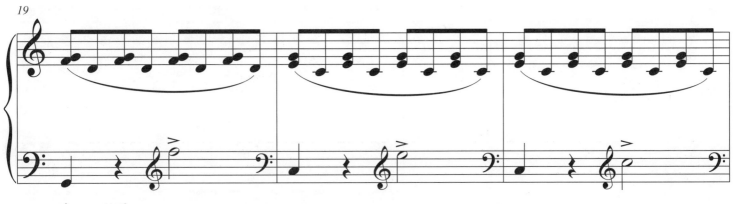

Night Escape
Op. 82, No. 65

Cornelius Gurlitt
(1820-1901)

Allegro non troppo

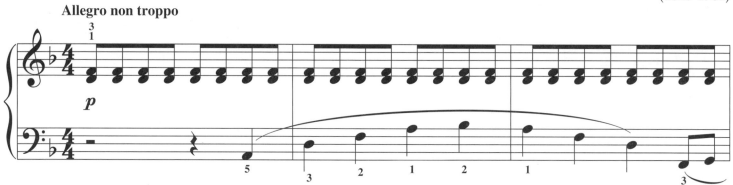

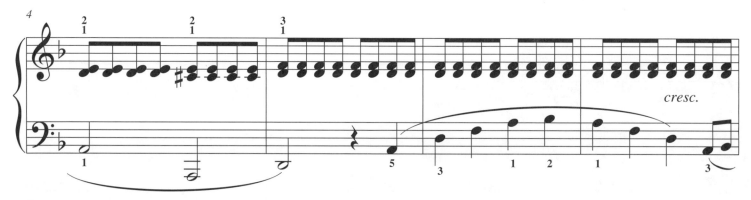

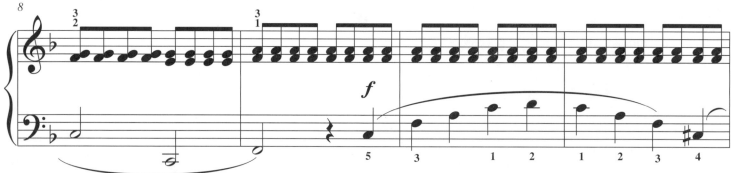